How to become a global citizen?

A Strategy for Change

Nurbek Achilov

Second Edition

Nurbek Achilov
How to become a Global Citizen: A Strategy for Change, 2019

2nd Edition
All Rights Reserved
ISBN: 9781670541581

Table of Content

Tables

Figures

I am dedicating this book to my children, who are very young to understand today's world disparities and challenges, but who are forming their thinking in new realities of globalization.

Globalization is a complex topic. It has its pros and cons. Despite that, I tried to explain it with my own words. I described my global actions based on my own experience in far regions of the country.

To adapt global changes, it is important to be persistent to learn new skills, form new thinking and prepare ourselves for new global actions. We have to educate our children and offspring on how to save water resources, how to keep our surroundings clean, how to act on a global level.

My experiences are not unique, but it provides our youth with new and unique ideas. These ideas help them think differently and bring new changes in areas where they live, study and work. Later, these young people can do far beyond their areas.

This special book will help to build a global mindset from small steps and start his or her global actions at a small pace.

Introduction

For many centuries, our humanity is in the fight for land, resources, and capital. Divided by more than 10 religious groups, 200 countries, thousands of languages and ethnic groups, we lost our global unity, efficiency, and development.

From aside, we simply live in the world of disparities, inefficiency and constant dilemmas. In the fight for natural and financial resources, our countries are still nationalistic, some are hegemonic and the others are religious. There are many states where dictatorship is prospering. They lead their countries in a way where the right solution has only the ruler. Not a community or majority of people have a voice or right to speak about its safety, common actions or development.

Today's demanding solution is a global mindset. And we, as national citizens, have to be global citizens to take over the issues and find new solutions.

The first aim of this handbook is to uncover a new type of person – a global citizen, its mission, principles, and actions. The second step is to show our challenging global and regional issues we face today and also many other topics, which our humanity can face in the future. The next aim is to describe the required actions of a global citizen to resolve our regional and global issues. The last point is to point out a number of features, which can help a global citizen to act and achieve the mission and goals.

The one interesting part of this book is to show a personal experience in the Turkestan region of how one could motivate local people for the global mindset and become global citizens. Just to note about the Turkestan region, it is in the heart of the Eurasian Continent and is far from the most developed regions.

Moreover, local citizens in the area were in isolation for more than 7 decades and under the propaganda of the Soviet information policy over 70 years. Before the Soviets, the region was under Tsarist Russia and khan ships, which fought with each other for centuries. They were from the same tribal groups but time and locations divided them into many languages and ways of statehood. These historic periods formed the most bureaucratic and inflexible mindset of people who are still facing difficulties, adapting to the market economy.

The idea was to motivate other readers to spread the voice of the global citizen via this handbook. With clear steps and recommendations, this book allows not only individuals but also organizations to change their understanding of the global citizen. To eliminate the fear of globalization, which many people despise in various countries, especially in those with strong national traditions, religions and single language policies.

This is also a motivational reading for young people to become global citizens in heart and in mind. The more and more global citizens can unite for global actions, the faster we can form our unique global culture together. That is the only way how we can effectively renovate our global infrastructure and economy.

As global citizens, we can achieve and do our changes uniting together and defending the future from random and venal decisions.

Who is the Global Citizen?

This is a question I ask myself for many years to find an exact definition.

Global Citizen, from my point of view, is an absolutely new type of personality who has new global values and traditions for understanding humankind as a single nation. It is a person with common values for living and working on our planet, without harmful effects on our nature, surroundings, and people.

Today, as citizens of various countries people divided by languages, histories, traditions, thinkings and national values. In many countries, people speak only their own local language with no interest to learn others. These circumstances create certain barriers for communication, common actions and efficiency.

Today, we have to ask ourselves: who am I? who I want to be? An isolated or nationalistic person or global citizen. A nationalist, who cares about his own national values and traditions, which are slowly disappearing or, on the other hand, a global citizen, who wants to find common values and advantages for development and efficiency. At the same time, a global citizen is the one who understands well and tries to apply the best practices of world history and culture.

Let me explain from my own experience. My interest in other cultures and economies was one of the reasons I tried to build my new principles from the world leaders. I looked for their motivating books, traveled to new destinations, organized international events, took part in a number of global activities, etc. Gradually, it formed my global mindset, which helped me to look at the same processes with a totally different mind and generate many ideas to turn other people in a right-thinking direction. For me, it was in areas of business, ecology, education, science, and many other areas.

I involved myself in the global institutions open for everyone. For example, I become a member of the Global Citizen Platform (the web-site at www.globalcitizen.org). This institution was a gateway for new ideas and the formation of my global culture.

Supporting various global activities, communicating with people around the world and writing on global topics, I have been forming global principles and points of view in people. Step by step, I understood that I formed a totally different global culture inside me. For the same situation and fact, I was looking with an absolutely different view – the eye of a Global Citizen.

It is not about a passport, which can certify about Global Citizenship or any other proven case. It is also not about Global Institutions, which you represent or involved as a member today. Till the moment, we do not have a global institution that evaluates people's global mindset and provide them with Global Citizenship. However, this is not a case to say that we cannot be a global citizen at all.

Living in any country of the world, with or without our national passport, we can be a true Global Citizen. The more and more Global Citizens will come the first in mind, the sooner the Global Institution will be created for certification of global citizens.

So, the Global Citizen today is a person who took global principles, values, traditions, and knowledge by heart and in mind, which can be seen in activities and actions a global citizen works every day.

In the period of dividing our communities into groups based on political views, social and economic statuses, it is hard to unite people for common actions on a global scale. Therefore, we cannot see and take action over our polluted oceans and environments in time. We will be always late in decision making. Because different groups used to create their own channels of influence, bureaucratize processes, and seed many restricting ideologies in people.

In many countries, those different leading groups are acting to:

1) Form nationalistic views and traditions;
2) Divide people based on race, nationality or citizenship;
3) Divide people based on religious or political views;
4) Create boundaries for free movement of people and migrants;
5) Prosecute opposition leaders, media and new thinkers;
6) Focus on developing enemies in the country and around;
7) Play on voters' expectations without any action for them in the future;
8) And others.

Today, on a regional level, many people do not care about what they breathe, eat and consume daily. Many people do not care about their health and offspring. They are isolated in many dimensions and do not care about other nations, the surrounding environment, our food supply and many other key points of human existence.

In many cases, their communication is limited. As they do not understand what global experts and scientists are speaking around the world about various global issues and trends. For sure, they need a single language or they need technology, which can instantly translate any language for understanding each other. However, even with the same language and unique technology in place, they cannot form the same values to act together. But they can communicate and gradually educate themselves to think in the same direction as global citizens. Thus, this means that anyone can become a global citizen with proper communication and education.

Generally, Global Citizens are those who can take one's thinking from limited thinking and conditions to a new level, uniting various groups of people to act together.

We can only unite with a global mindset in heart and mind. It can help us to unite our intentions and actions into a global movement. This can make our relationships stronger and powerful, especially in overcoming the most difficult issues of the regional and global agendas.

In fact, globalization is our new future and our duty to prepare people, especially, offspring to move the progress further. They have to learn how to cope with many barriers to communication, thinking, values, multiple traditions, etc. They have to learn to create common values too. And it is about education in family and primary/secondary schools.

Without being a global citizen, we cannot simply educate our children to adapt them to global trends. We cannot talk and explain to them how they have to communicate with other nations.

And this book is a starting point to change and motivate our communities for a new direction. It should become a handbook to start changes in mindset and create global citizens in the heart.

This should also motivate globalists to write literature on specific issues, especially on Global Government and Global Citizenship, which can be open access online to any person who passes certain criteria for global actions.

This question I asked myself decades ago when I had a wish to study abroad and make the first contribution to the economic development of the region and the global economy.

I was not a unique student or person. I was without any gadgets or technology. And I was without any experienced supporters nearby who could direct me in my global vision. Imagine now how many times this could increase my efficiency of work and intentions if I would have a laptop 25-30 years back, for example?

So, the interesting question is: how could I become a global citizen without any gadgets or technology, or uniqueness?

After reviewing myself and the period of changes, I defined several key factors. They are:

- Language
- Upbringing
- Education
- Principles
- Global Missions
- Global Actions

Let me briefly explain how these factors helped me to become a global citizen.

Languages

At home, I speak Kazakh. At school, I used to speak Russian. And, in the yard, Uzbek Language. From a very young age, my father taught me English, for example, starting how to count or say greetings, etc.

It helped me to receive information easily from various sources and communicate easily, on the one hand, and to build my interest in other languages, on the other.

After I entered university, I started to read professional books in English and German. My early English and multi-language character gave me so many advantages in learning and exploring new areas.

When I started my professional work, I was very interested to understand other cultures, their thinking, and values. I started to learn Japanese, Chinese and other languages to succeed at understanding different cultures, values, and traditions.

Generally, languages helped me to access progressive information faster, effectively and to a certain extent in a wide range of topics, which were not covered in post-soviet countries.

Till the moment, I consider a language as a communication and learning tool. In fact, no other factor provides so wide access to learning cultures, traditions and many other differences we have among countries, social groups, etc.

So, the first starting point is language. It is important to learn the English Language today to access global information sources in various fields. It is also about communication. For example, with English, you can talk to people almost everywhere in the world.

So, the first languages to learn are:

1) English
2) Turan (the basic language of all Turk speaking nations or regions like Kazakhstan, Uzbekistan, Tadjikistan, Kyrgyzstan, Tatarstan, Turkey, Azerbaijan and etc. There are many who speak in West China, Iran, Afghanistan, Hungary and etc.)
3) Russian
4) Arabic
5) French
6) German
7) Spanish
8) Chinese

But language is not the only factor, which drives a person's global mindset. For example, there are billions of people, who speak English around the world, however, they have limited understanding of the global issues, cultures and are careless about global trends and problems.

Upbringing

There are many skills, knowledge, and experiences, you can only learn in your family. Family is a powerful source for supporting, motivating and developing one's character.

Your father and mother, grandparents, brothers and sisters, other relatives are contributors to your character. Only in the family, you can learn how to behave, respect, share, and love. Only in the family you understand your identity, learn values and traditions and listen to true stories about the past, people and ancestors.

For example, I was lucky to spend some time with my grandfather and listened to his stories about Germany, France, Italy and other countries at a very young age. It formed my interest and dreams about the countries, which I visited later in my life.

Further, I also learned many important lessons and evaluations from my grandparents. They were the only source I could understand many mistakes of other people in learning and acting, including my parents and other elder people around. So, it formed a certain character that I have never grown the bad habits no matter of circumstances.

Moreover, my grandfather taught me how to plant a tree in the yard, saying how important trees for bringing fruits and oxygen for people.

Abovementioned shows that we have to care about children and especially what kind of information and care they receive in their babyhood and during the school years, vacations.

Today, many children grow up in orphanages and many with parents without basic upbringing and education about nature, people around.

The main areas for children to understand are:

1) Countries
2) Nationalities
3) Religions
4) Cultures
5) United Nations
6) Nature
7) Ecology
8) Plants
9) Animals
10) Wastes
11) People
12) Races
13) others

The number one priority in upbringing is to prepare global citizens from a young age. And build their interest in many areas of our global agenda.

Education

The next important factor is education.

If stopped my education with a school or bachelor's degree, I would never have a chance to become a global citizen in the heart and actions.

Education helps to level up all the skills and requirements, including for English, thinking, vision, competences and other skills necessary to work in a professional way.

When it is about global knowledge, it is important to understand that anyone can become a true global citizen at any age, no matter the past life.

Life-long education is one of the solutions, which can balance human imperfections and lack of skills by targeted content and programs of education for any age group.

The priority is to evaluate the person's horizon of thinking and actions, which can fit into the level of global actions. For example, the majority of people around the world are not interested in global matters. They think that they have to resolve their social and economic issues first. And, on the other side, they believe that global issues are far from their reality. They have to think about how to find food for today or for their babies.

If we look at it from an international perspective, any local issue is a global issue. For example, lack of food in one country can be resolved if people, who live in that country, to understand that in another country the food is in abundance. Or a high level of poverty and unemployment in one country are pushing people to think locally, for example, to earn their daily money only. But when they are educated, they will think about many ideas and solutions on how to increase their sources of income. For example, they can learn how to create high-value products and use advantages for exporting new products, for example, via e-commerce tools.

Therefore, a number one task is to focus on life-long education which can train people at any age on how to be a global citizen.

For global citizen, it is important to build programs in the following fields:

1) Geography;
2) World History;
3) International Relations;
4) International Business;
5) Cross-Cultural Management;
6) Waste Management;
7) Strategic Management;
8) Others.

These main areas of education that will form interlinks between many areas and sectors of the economies.

Principles

Any person to cultivate public or build personal principles. Many of these principles change during a lifespan, but core principles are for the whole life.

The best thing about the principles, they can be changed over time based on new experiences, knowledge, and circumstances.

For a global citizen, it is important to build the following principles as a priority:

1) Be open mind. It means that a person should be open to any new idea to discuss, accept or think critically.
2) Think global – adjust locally. For any issue, one has to think globally but adjust new ideas to the budget, mindset, and other local circumstances.
3) Motivate yourself for learning. Diplomas and certificates keep everyone out of the books and further education. A person should practice self-motivation for continuous learning.
4) Be punctual. Time is the main economic resource for development. Lack of punctuality wastes time, especially of others.
5) Stay honest on all issues and activities. Trust between people becomes stronger when people work, talk and act honestly. It should be cultivated at a young age.
6) Keep fairness in decision making and allocation. No state or company can grow without fairness in place.
7) Be a person of the word. If you promise, do your best to finish your work or return what you had taken.
8) Take responsibility as a priority. Nothing is valuable than responsibility, especially, when it comes to the realization of plans.

9) Others.

The principles are the only source of human motivation that can drive a person for knowledge on a constant base.

Global Mission

I always ask myself how people will live in the destroyed, depleted and polluted environment in the coming 100 years.

Our humankind has already done so much and there are a lot of examples of the environments with no living conditions. For example, dried out the Aral Sea area. Here, the catastrophe still grows bigger and bigger and influences more areas. I learned that it influenced more than 500 kilometers from the area. Especially, sandy winds which have been bringing salty Aral sands new areas year by year.

The lesson is that we are far from understanding that tomorrow we have to live on this planet and catch fish in the rivers, plant crops in the land, etc.

Once I formulated my own global mission to do my best to change people's attitudes and character. I decided to change people's mindset toward nature, ecology, wastes and global issues. I also connected all these to financial, economic, social benefits, etc.

I understood that I am not the only person in the world and at least I can do my best in the country where I am living and can benefit millions of people. So, I started it from Kazakhstan and Central Asia.

Joining the Astana Economic Forum I was organizing the first forum of 300 participants. In a few years, with a global approach, we could unite more than 12 000 delegates and participants in one platform. The faith helped me to convince many top managers and government people in the direction of the Astana Economic Forum and the internet platform, which was a connecting element of annual forums. The ideas of the internet platform were to discuss global issues on a constant base, long before participants could meet in the Astana Economic Forum. Later, the President of the country transformed our internet platform into the G-Global Info-communication Platform. It ran discussions about the topics of the coming Astana Economic Forum, becoming a connecting point of annual forums.

This allowed us to gather recommendations and prepare the final outcomes of the forum to present them annually to the United Nations, G-20 leaders and other global institutions.

My global mission has never stopped, even after I left the organizing committee of the Astana Economic Forum.

I understood that this mission still drives me to areas where other people and leaders have never looked at. After moving to a provincial Shymkent city, my global mission helped me to uncover the advantages of the region from a different angle – a global perspective.

Based on observations and analysis, I developed recommendations and reports connecting local cities such as Shymkent and Turkestan to the Great Silk Road Concept, the past history of khan ships including the Chinggis khan and Tamerlane and also to the followers of the prophet Mahomed. I showed how important are the cities for global trade between East and West and also for global tourism, as in Mausoleum in Turkestan city, not only the Khodja Ahmed was engraved, but also more than 300 descendants of the Chinggis khan.

During the Soviet period, the vast territory of the khans was divided in the Soviet Republics. And in the near past, each ruler in the republic was thinking that he is the one who has the most power. It created many barriers between countries, especially between Kazakhstan and Uzbekistan, Uzbekistan and Tajikistan, Uzbekistan and Kyrgyzstan. I did my best to provide information for governors of the countries to change the thinking from a global perspective and from past history.

My Global Mission helped me to see the most difficult issues of the region from a totally different angle – again a global perspective. Making our problems so tiny before the global issues which require more efforts to unite nations for common actions.

Global Actions

When a person has a limited view or has never thought about issues from a global perspective, a person will act based on personal values, local traditions, and hardships. No matter the position, social status or income a person will be selfish, nationalistic or narrow-minded in many issues.

Global actions are the actions that are done based on global perspectives, issues, and understanding of the outcomes for global communities. It requires specific knowledge to act critically, absorb new ideas, lessen difficult situations and influence people in a positive way.

There are four areas where we can apply global actions: 1) personal issues 2) local issues; 3) regional issues and 4) global issues.

Let's see how we apply global actions on personal issues. In the first example, everyone wants to be the best specialist. If a person lives with local understanding and actions, he will probably end up in the school. But if a person acts on a personal issue with global actions, he will end up with a doctoral degree or an international degree.

The second example is the job place. If a person acts locally, he will end up in the company with a narrow market and scope. But if a person applies and works in the company with global actions, his or her company will go with its products or services beyond the borders of the region, country or continent.

How to apply global actions on local issues. For example, if we take drying out Aral see with local actions we will end up with paperwork and no positive changes in the lives of local people. For example, in areas around Aral see people struggle from lack of water, salty winds, and sandstorms. And no single government program can support them till now.

When we can do it with global actions on local problems of the Aral Sea, we can demonstrate the most devasting case for the whole world, especially those who are living in the cities and better climate conditions. With global actions, we can draw the attention of millions of people for support and taking actions, especially in regard to local government activities and budget allocation. Global actions can push local governments to work effectively and provide support for local people in their migration or receiving their social benefits.

The same with regional and global issues. Global actions can resolve the most dangerous and ecological issues with the support of the global community. For example, owners of the ships and sea boats, which throw daily millions of tons of garbage will hide their activities and this will be unnoticeable for people who live far from ports, islands, or seashores. They can only understand the problems and effects of the tankers or waste boats from people with global actions only.

Our mission for global actions has no limit on the application. We can act with global actions on any issue of our community. Let's see some other examples of the classification of global actions.

First, regarding personal issues which can be classified as the following:

1) Providing life-long education for all;
2) Developing the products or services for multinational markets;
3) Resolving psychological or social problems of women and children;
4) Eliminating gender inequality;
5) Creating unique artworks etc.

In regard to local issues, they include areas such as:

1) Unemployment and job creation;
2) Educating people;
3) Developing rural areas;
4) Resolving poverty issues;
5) Stability from Inflation;
6) Green Construction;
7) Home services etc.

These local issues, if resolved with global actions can be resolved easily. For example, today the unemployment issues resolved by creating a production line under old financial schemes or technologies. The same with educating people. In many countries, universities are educating youth with specializations, which are not demanding anymore. From a global perspective, according to many international experts, more than 100 specializations will disappear in the near future, but at the same time, more than 150 new specializations will be created and demanding. So, if the local government will push its new programs for creating absolutely new ventures with demanding specializations, then they will stimulate local people to learn new specializations. And it is clear that colleges and universities will follow the trend.

Regional issues are complex in terms of country-driven or ethnic driven issues. From the perspective of Asian or European countries, they include:

1) Drying out Aral see;
2) The annexation of Crimea;
3) Uighurs and Muslim Rights in China;
4) Ukraine and Russia tensions;
5) US and China Trade War;
6) India and Pakistan tensions;
7) Afghanistan's war and peace issues;
8) Sanctions on Iran and Russia;
9) Separatism in Spain and Russia;
10) Effects of Chernobyl on East Europe;
11) Iran and its nuclear project;
12) Syria ethnic fight;
13) Brexit;
14) Border tensions etc.

In some way, these complex issues are limited with one or several countries and in many cases they are regional. The only problem is that they are now resolved with local and regional approaches, based on ideas and comments of local people.

From a global perspective, for example, if all countries of the region will understand the effects of the drying out of the Aral sea on glaciers, water resources and health of people in Tajikistan, Kyrgyzstan, Uzbekistan, and Kazakhstan, they will take different approaches in regard to agriculture, irrigation systems and water-supply systems.

In regard to Annexed Crimea is an issue of destroying the life of not Ukrainians, but according to many experts, the life of the Crimean Tatars, who cannot receive their republican status because of Stalin policy on nations, who served Hitler's Regime during World War II. But it happened more than 70 years ago. And now absolutely new generations of people are living in the peninsula and around the world. There is a big question: should we live on policies of past history or new future perspectives?

Again, if this regional issue is taken from a global perspective, the issue will be resolved easily. Crimean Tatars have their ancestors from Turks, Russians, Germans, and many other nations. They have no single gene, which belongs to one nation. So, there is no point of doing ethnic or country policy over the Crimea for politicians. If the local people want to be independent or be in the part of one country, they have to decide themselves, not Russia, Ukraine or Turkey or any country in the world.

Unfortunately, today, global issues are also resolved with local or regional approaches. Therefore, we have so many barriers to interconnection and common global efficiency. Nations understand and fight for land, and they are careless in regard to oceans, nature, ecology and the most terribly for the life of their people, their families and themselves, and most importantly for their offspring. That's because people evaluate the wealth of today as possession of something. It can be a land, people, paper money or some other valuables.

We have to accept that many of our previous and present generations have never thought about the global trends and issues to work on them.

That's why our humanity has so many wars in the past and present, drying out of Aral sea, nuclear bomb tests, Chernobyl catastrophe in Ukraine, melting of glaciers because of climate change and many other ecological outcomes.

Actually, until now, there is no clear classification of global trends and issues in full scope. Probably it is a big topic of new research for us together.

Despite that, let's try to classify our main global issues and trends below as a preliminary step:

1) Climate change;
2) Pollution of the air;
3) Pollution of underwater and oceans;
4) Pollution of products;
5) Pollution of orbit;
6) Waste Land fields and Management;
7) Epidemics and healthcare;
8) GMO and other ingredients;
9) Extreme Poverty;
10) Drainage and water supply systems;
11) Food supply and systems;
12) Illegal Migration and Traffic;
13) Global Energy Networks and Sources;
14) Global Security and National Disarmament;
15) Nuclear and Radiation Security;
16) Personal Security Protection;
17) Global Financial Architecture and Currencies;
18) Global Economy and Entrepreneurship;
19) Dictatorships and Democratic Elections;
20) Global Citizenship;
21) New technologies and patents;
22) Outdated education;
23) Global Networks and Roads;
24) Human Rights;
25) Nationalism;
26) Corruption;
27) Terrorism;
28) Exploration of cosmos;
29) Exploration of earth and many other;

From a global perspective, there are many issues that require the involvement of all nations in a chain of common actions. There are many platforms like Global Citizen or G-Global Info-Communication Platform, which raise and discuss the issues, call for global actions on the one side. And organizations such as the United Nations, OSCE, CICA, and many other organizations, on the other side. They all work on global issues and call for actions. But they are limited in terms of executive power.

From the analysis, I could see several issues:

1) Power of interest. With an only country interest in mind, it is impossible to drive global issues for a result.
2) Corruption. According to some experts of the UN, many programs are realized with corrupted networks of diplomats and country leaders.
3) Geopolitics. Many experts note that some leading countries want to control the countries and territories which were their colonies in the 17-19 centuries.
4) Science. Using science and development as an instrument of trade wars and controlling the markets.
5) Local thinking. Many areas and countries of the world are still blocked from the internet, information access, and free trade.
6) Others.

There are many platforms, where leaders of countries meet together to resolve their policies and agree on single ones for effective collaboration. However, that's not enough. There are only around 100 main global leaders around the world. And they work in their specific areas: politics, business, media, etc. International relations and global collaboration are the areas where we can see not leaders, but more experts, diplomats, and politicians who are working in the interest of their countries.

That's the main point, why global citizens are demanding to solve global issues with their global actions. This is also the point why we can grow global leaders – global citizens effectively take the most active role in different parts of the world. They can effectively understand the global trends and issues and lead their countries and nations toward common global actions.

Today we can solve our global issues as global citizens only. Global citizens are the new leaders of our global era. Only they can lead their nations to meet the challenging issues and unite for global actions.

Here, it is important also to classify two types of global trends.

First, the trends, which are consequences of human activity. For example,

-climate change,

-waste landfills,

-ocean waste,

-country-specific and regional riots,

-global trade wars,

-excavation of natural resources,

-political disputes and debates,

-epidemics,

-migration,

-human rights,

-drying out of rivers, lakes, and seas,

-and others.

Second, global trends which are consequences of human activity, limited natural resources or technological changes. For example,

-digitalization of the countries,

-robotization of economies and industries,

-development of alternative sources of energy,

-artificial intelligence management systems,

-big data centers,

-implementation of green technologies,

-regional and global integration of transportation, logistics, and other systems,

-development of global cryptocurrencies,

-integration of markets for wholesale and retail,

-exchange programs between countries,

-etc.

Global trends help us to understand new opportunities for global actions. They help global leaders where to focus, adapt and how to resolve those key issues timely.

On the country and rural levels, it is important that governments work on their policies integrating them into global policies. Generally, global politics is a new instrument that can accelerate the process of forming global citizens for actions and resolving global issues in the country and rural areas.

Global Politics

Many authors explain that global politics is a study to find the positive traits and relationships between countries for collaboration and development, as well as for effective management of resources.

But, actually, it is not a full understanding of global politics. Because, many countries build their policies and politics exceptionally based on their local interests, or interests of a limited group of people to manipulate and control the natural and financial resources of their countries.

That's the truth of today's national politics. No matter the size of the country or its intentions to globalize.

Global Politics, in fact, should be a foundation of the countries to follow global rules and work for uniting the global community and actions. They have to research together to find areas for common work and cooperation.

It requires countries to develop and accept a single global constitution, legal documents such as Global Trust Agreement. For example, most nations that have the same history, traditions and languages can fight with each other because of their territorial borders, which were divided by colonial countries of the 19th century, Soviet Union or during the Cold War between the US and USSR. These vulnerable countries should be brought together on a trust agreement first. They have to understand their true history and geopolitical intentions of the politicians in some countries.

As a good example, there are long-lasting trends on a regional level, for example in the EU, Eurasian Economic Union and other regions.

On a global level, it will require to consider issues that are far beyond the country's borders. For example, for Kazakhstan – it can be relationships with countries of Africa, Latin America or Australia.

The difficulty of global politics is hidden in its way how countries can interact with each other without roads, networks or trade connections.

And here comes the wisdom of global politics – global economics. What does it mean?

For example, on a global level, each country has its own competitive advantage. For example, in Kazakhstan, we cannot produce a banana as in the subtropical countries. Or Brazil has no competitive advantage like Kazakhstan in connecting Europe with Asia via land or connecting Russia with the Middle East.

The next point is about understanding the main factors. There are several caterpillars of global politics and they are:

- adoption of a global constitution;

- acceptance of global rules;

- prioritizing the global interest of all communities rather than local interests;

- building strategies for growing global citizens;

- understanding the competitive advantage of the country in the global arena;

- defining the level of contribution of global citizens of the country for the global economy;

- promoting global education for global citizens;

- increasing the number of global citizens of the country;

- others;

Moreover, in the following table let me show the main elements of national and global politics.

Table 1 Comparison of National and Global Politics

Priorities	National	Global
Country Programs	National, based on the interest of limited groups, ethnical or tribal unions, etc.	Global, based on interest including the interest of neighbor countries
Border policy	Closed, controlled, custom control zones	Open, crime control zones
Global Citizen Requirements	No, restricted	Yes, including global institutions for education, research, testing and issuing global citizen documentation or certification
Constitution	National, based on national values and traditions	Global, based on global values, issues, and trends, including national advantages
Identity	Nationality, Ethnics, Social Status	Knowledge, Education, Citizenship
Currency policy	The national currency, exchange	National and global currencies, cryptocurrencies
Human rights	Respected to supporters and party	Respected to all, including minorities and global citizens
Market rules	The power of sellers, bankers, and governors	The power of customer and consumers
Competitive Advantage	Access to finance and resources of limited groups, media coverage, territory or other elements	Education and science, R&D, transparency of wealth distribution, the national economic competitiveness of geo-location and human resources
Values for Growth	Contacts, Tribal or Local Links and Connections, Corruption, Exceptional Random Contribution	Global Knowledge, Experience, Publications, Research, Purposeful Contribution, etc.

The table gives an understanding of the importance to transform countries from national politics to global politics.

It includes many important priorities to consider to form a truly global environment that will support global citizens for greater contributions.

The table also includes the important elements of global economics, markets, and other sectors, we have to uncover in the sections below.

Global Economics

In many sources, global economics tries to understand the global output, trade, export, and import. It is our economic relations and it forms a basic understanding of global economics from a national point of view.

But I believe when we talk about global economics, we have to understand the following elements first:

1) Global Population as a global human force;
2) Global Resources as a capacity for global growth;
3) Global Time as a man-hour measure and productivity;
4) Global Currency as a unit of income and expenditures of the global economy;
5) Global Output as a measure of global efficiency and growth.

For clearness, let me design the following comparison table.

Table 2 Comparison of National and Global Economics

Priorities	National Economics	Global Economics
Workforce	Priority to the workforce with national skills	Priority to the workforce with national and global skills
Time	Depends on cultural values	Valuable resource for global efficiency
Resources	National wealth	Source of global competitiveness and effectiveness
Currency	The symbol of national independence, payment	Source of saving, wealth, payment and investment
Trade: Export/Import	Source of national income and growth	Source of global competitive advantage
State Program	Improvement of National Competitiveness	Improvement of Global Competitive Advantage and Workforce
Ecological Issues	Within Border	Beyond Border
Legal Framework	National	Based on international values and best practices for fairness and human rights
Personal Information and Accounts	Vulnerable to State and Private Access and Infringements	Confidential to anybody, organization or person

Infrastructure	Exchange, Banks, Trade houses, Embassies, Governments	Global Platforms, Blockchain, E-commerce, Global Exchange, Global Payment Wallets, Cryptocurrencies

The table above provides ideas for the deliberate process of decision making for global economics. In the context of global development, they have many challenging barriers. But they are so important to prioritize. Let's check the main elements out in detail.

Global Population and Time

At a global level, we divide the population for many nationalities, boundaries, ethnic groups, and so many other elements. And when it comes to the global population, we cannot explain how we are going to solve global population issues in the mid and long term.

From my understanding, if we have 7 billion of citizens around the world, we know that there are 3,5 billion of the workforce, who can work in different positions. They are the most powerful workforce of our planet. Among them, there are many who are educated or who are illiterate. No matter of their educational level, we should understand the following arithmetic calculation for global efficiency.

Let's calculate the total number of work hours per day. If each person works 8 hours per day, the total sum of work hours is equal: 3,5 billion citizens * 8 hours/citizens = 28 billion hours per day.

For one year, it is around 10,22 trillion hours/year.

From a global perspective, we can use this valuable time for anything that can make our world more efficient in many areas of global development. Imagine if every person will spend 1 hour a day on cleaning a planet. We will rid of all waste in just one week.

For that, we have to define the global work volume and the measurement of currency per hour. It is important that the payment scheme is fair, clear and in time.

Global Currency and Capital

Analyzing that we have limited hours per year, we can plan effectively the work amount and the volume of capital on a global scale. So, it will help to accelerate the development and motivation of countries for new steps of progress.

If an average person will get USD 50 per hour, so the total volume of capital required for the global economy is USD 511 trillion.

So, it is understandable that if the GDP of the World Economy according to International Monetary Fund in 2019 is around USD 142 trillion, the rest of the capital will go for saving and investing future projects.

From a different angle, it shows that each working person in the world (from 3,5 billion of the workforce) is contributing on average for the World GDP with the amount of USD13,8 per working hour.

Generally, it shows that on the global level, there are many people, who work too much to produce global wealth and there are many, who do not work at all. This shows that global efficiency will be based on the creation of additional value by involving all unemployed part of the global workforce.

Global Resources

Our planet resources are limited and we do not know what consequences the planet can face because of the extraction of natural resources from under the earth. We do not know how it will affect the circulation of our earth in the cosmos and generally for the magnetic field or ozone shield of our planet.

Natural resources should be understood and evaluated not as a resource for extraction but for their role for the existence of our planet, balancing the earth's trajectory of movement around the sun and many other features.

These issues are out of the topic of the national governments and national organizations, which are focusing more on national interests of countries for 5-10 years at maximum. They do not care about how the planet will live in 50-100 years. What will be the conditions of climate and land for offspring and other living beings and for growing on the planet?

Without efforts of global institutions and global governance, it is impossible to change the situation. The world needs some urgent actions for it. And we have to put our efforts to create a global government.

Global Government

Many organizations work on a global level to resolve global issues. They are mainly financed by multinational companies or leading countries to solve their own issues.

The United Nations is one of the key structures for financing global projects too. But it again limited that is based on national interests and works on consequences.

On a global scale, we have also international financial institutions, international funds, and unions such as the European Union, which are financing many global projects for developing the regions. But again, the results of this organizations are difficult to evaluate and unseen. And most importunately, the policies are developed based on the union's interests for the long and midterm future.

Several years back I was developing a model of global governance as one of the key experts of the Eurasian Economic Club of Scientists (see Figure below). It was a thoughtful structure with many elements and relations to the present global institutions. That time cryptocurrencies were not in the media and the idea was to return to the gold standard on a global level. But anyway, it was not interesting to any of the governors as it required some efforts to unite nations.

Even though the idea of the structure is still demanding and for implementation of such a global scale project we need a more powerful institution that can control, govern globally and regulate currency volume.

It was 5 years back. But, now we see the rise of cryptocurrencies and at the same time the active position of such institutions such as Global Citizen, and many other global organizations.

And as an outcome, there is a question, what kind of global government we need now.

From my own point of view, Global Government should be based on the following:

1) The legitimacy of the country;
2) Adoption of the global constitution;
3) Acceptance of the global currencies, including cryptocurrencies;
4) Respect for national boundaries and cultures;
5) Creation of the global parliament;
6) Development of the global bank and payment system etc.

These are not easy tasks, but it will help to create an infrastructure for the growth of global citizens in any country in the world.

There are many skeptics and opponents of the global government, in fact. It is understandable that countries want to have more power and control their resources and capital on their own. In fact, even today, national governments are focused only on the benefits of the target activities for their countries.

The idea of creating governments was in the effective management of resources and creating competition between countries. But it did not work. There was so much in the history that some leaders behaved like kings, some tribal rulers behaved that they need more land, some leaders started to humiliate other nations and minorities.

When we talk about the global marketplace, global government is more an issue of the global communities to take an active role in realizations of global actions.

For global actions, a person can be a citizen of any country, regardless of race, nationality, religion and etc.

So, the true idea was to form a global citizen. Only could global citizens take many people from national thinking to a level of global thinking and global government.

Without creating a quick global structure it is impossible to move global actions in all corners at the same time.

Compared to the United Nations Organization, multinational companies are more productive in moving their products and services, and social programs more effectively in any corner of the world.

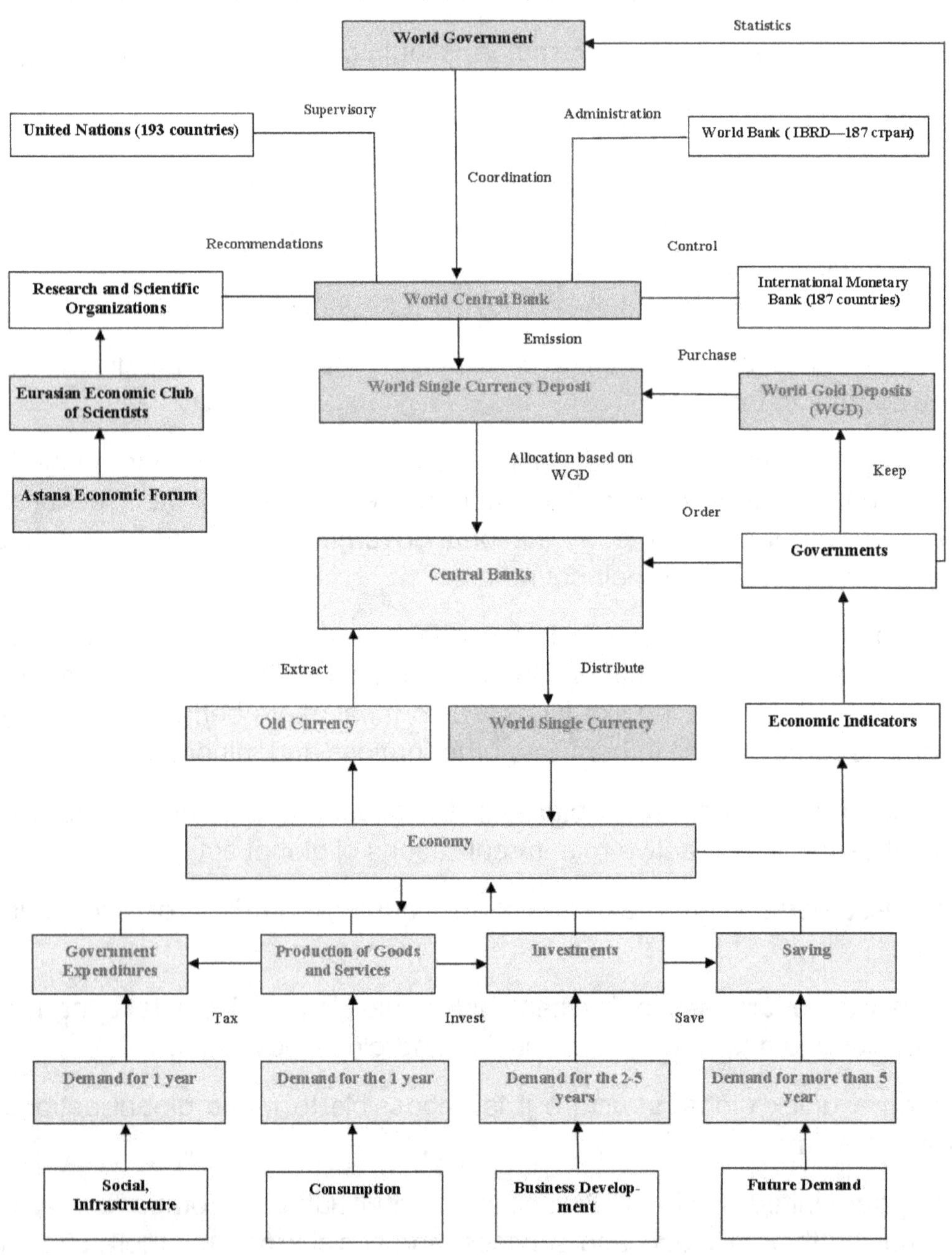
PROPOSAL OF EURASIAN ECONOMIC CLUB OF SCIENTISTS
IN THE V ASTANA ECONOMIC FORUM

MECHANISMS OF DEVELOPMENT OF NEW WORLD FINANCIAL SYSTEM
AND THE NEW WORLD CURRENCY

World Government
Statistics
United Nations (193 countries)
Supervisory
Administration
World Bank (IBRD—187 стран)
Coordination
Recommendations
Control
Research and Scientific Organizations
World Central Bank
International Monetary Bank (187 countries)
Emission
Purchase
Eurasian Economic Club of Scientists
World Single Currency Deposit
World Gold Deposits (WGD)
Astana Economic Forum
Allocation based on WGD
Keep
Order
Central Banks
Governments
Extract
Distribute
Old Currency
World Single Currency
Economic Indicators
Economy
Government Expenditures
Production of Goods and Services
Investments
Saving
Tax
Invest
Save
Demand for 1 year
Demand for the 1 year
Demand for the 2-5 years
Demand for more than 5 year
Social, Infrastructure
Consumption
Business Development
Future Demand
©Eurasian Economic Club of Scientists

From a practical point, we see that global institutions, businesses, and international organizations are ready to cooperate to improve the situation in a certain country with a limited focus on cross-national projects. However, most of them are ready only on those projects, which have a guaranteed financial mechanism for the realization of the actions by the local governments. Of course, with such kind of approach, we cannot resolve and clean fully our oceans, for example, which has no controlling owner or government.

In addition, a national citizen will never agree to pay a tax in order to accumulate the funds for the creation of the global government. Moreover, governments do not want to pay additional contributions when they pay for membership in the United Nations Organizations and many other international organizations.

So, building a global government requires the following:

1) Step by step plan of actions;
2) Unification of rules;
3) Unification of standards;
4) Unification of business etiquette;
5) Unification of infrastructure;
6) Unification of public areas;
7) Acceptance of single currency and cryptocurrencies;
8) Creation of institutions with sources of global funding;
9) Fair allocation of funds;
10) Others

There are many barriers and issues which decrease the legitimacy of the global government in practice. Especially without the financial system.

Therefore, the idea was to start a global government, which can be started in a virtual global environment, developed with the purpose of bringing global citizens for contribution in the electronic environment.

E-Global Government

E-Global Government can be an initial stage of creating a Global Government in practice.

Global Citizens can join from any place where they have internet access. And E-Global Government can be a place where Global Citizens can join under special terms and rules to act and support global actions, create their own cryptocurrency for supporting their actions or take the existing cryptocurrencies. They can also elect their E-Global Parliament and E-Global Government providing certain quotes for countries and rotating their leaders in the positions in the E-Global Parliament and E-Global Government.

To make the system of E-Global Government working, the main requirements can be based on experiences of unions of governments. For example, in order to become a member of the E-Global Government, for each specific position, there should be a voting system based on a quota for each country.

In addition, members and interested governments can create a budget on the blockchain with a specific purpose to finance the projects of the E-Global Government on a global scale, where any member or global citizen can take part as a specialist, volunteer or intern.

In other words, E-Global Government will work as a system, which unites the functionalities of such systems like Facebook, Cryptocurrency Wallets and E-Gov Platforms of many countries.

This platform will help to bring a new type of citizens – Global Citizens, who can contribute effectively to the development of their countries and the global economy.

The important part is a global infrastructure, which should serve effectively the system and defend global citizens from any prejudices, local manipulations, corruption, etc.

Global Infrastructure

Global Infrastructure should save time, effectively allocate global resources or unite global citizens in the projects and at the same time defend them from any violation of their rights and principles.

We have to understand that the infrastructure is dependent on many other areas such as Transport, Engineering, Geography, IT, Communication, Legal System, Human Rights, Budgeting, Food Security, Ecology, Quality Management, Global Supply Chain Management, Global Governance, and many others.

Globally, the topic is more discussed in the context of global and international businesses, but in the context of a global infrastructure for global citizens, there is no information and appropriate infrastructure, which is only discussed in the context of global tourism infrastructure.

Therefore, I would like to focus on several key concepts to draw the main points of global infrastructure development.

Global Food Security

According to many international sources, there are more than 2 billion people live in poverty and hunger. It is around 30% of the world population.

Several years ago, I had a chance to prepare a strategic roadmap for food security and placed it in many sources.

The figure of the section is an outcome of discussions and brainstorming about global food security where we can see a complex mechanism for global food security infrastructure.

The realization of such a project requires a lot of effort for agreeing with many details with every country and it takes years for looking for investments.

As I showed this concept and shared it in Kazakhstan, the country has the key advantage to focus on its food security infrastructure and network. On a country level, it was quite fast to start the preliminary steps for implementation.

Even though it was slow, but in many regional centers of Kazakhstan, now we have warehouses and food stability funds. It helps local people access high quality and fresh products, including vegetables and fruits, with the best price.

Figure 2 Roadmap for Ensuring Food Security

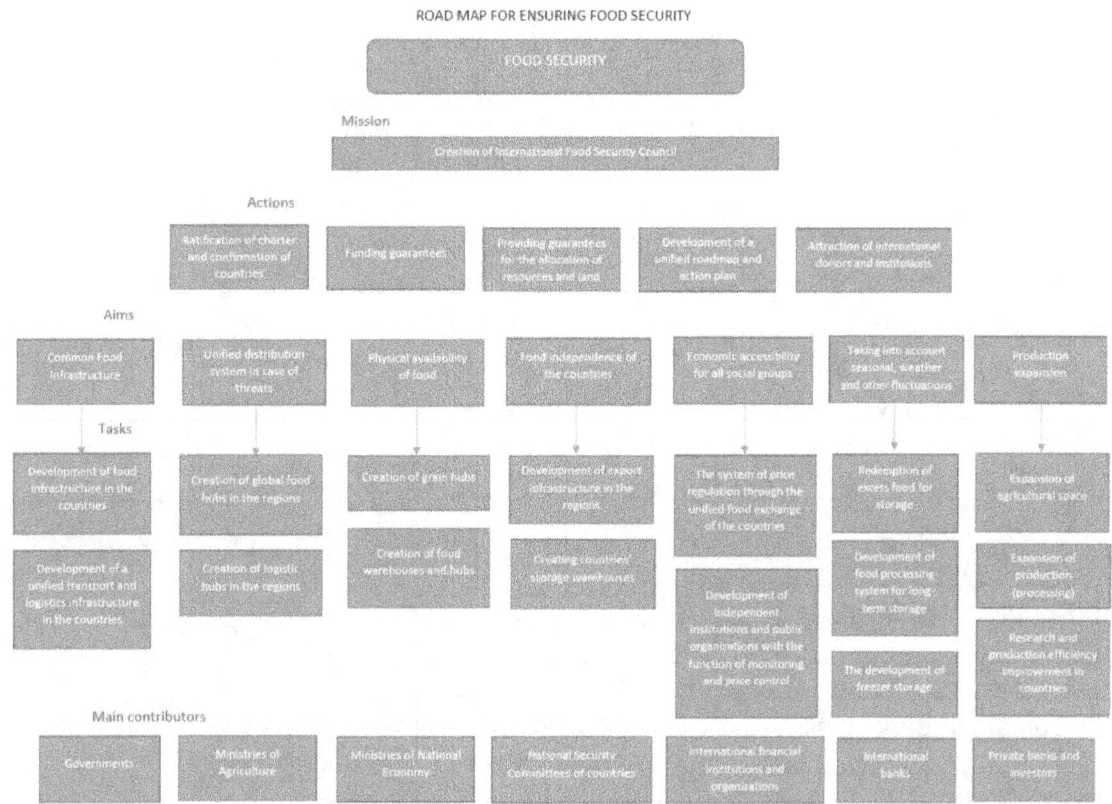

This concept can move the global food security infrastructure and help the global community to create stability funds and infrastructure in the period of global climate change.

To realize a global infrastructure for global citizens, it is important to develop a concept or roadmap for local governments that can support the idea on a country level first.

Global Ecology and Waste

Based on the analysis and design of the systems of several countries, in my book "Waste Management: From Concept to Action Plan" I described many models for waste management.

Without this concept, it was not easy to explain the topic to many green leaders of the country. And when it was launched, I placed it in the internet forums of the Astana Economic Forum and other platforms to discuss it with experts.

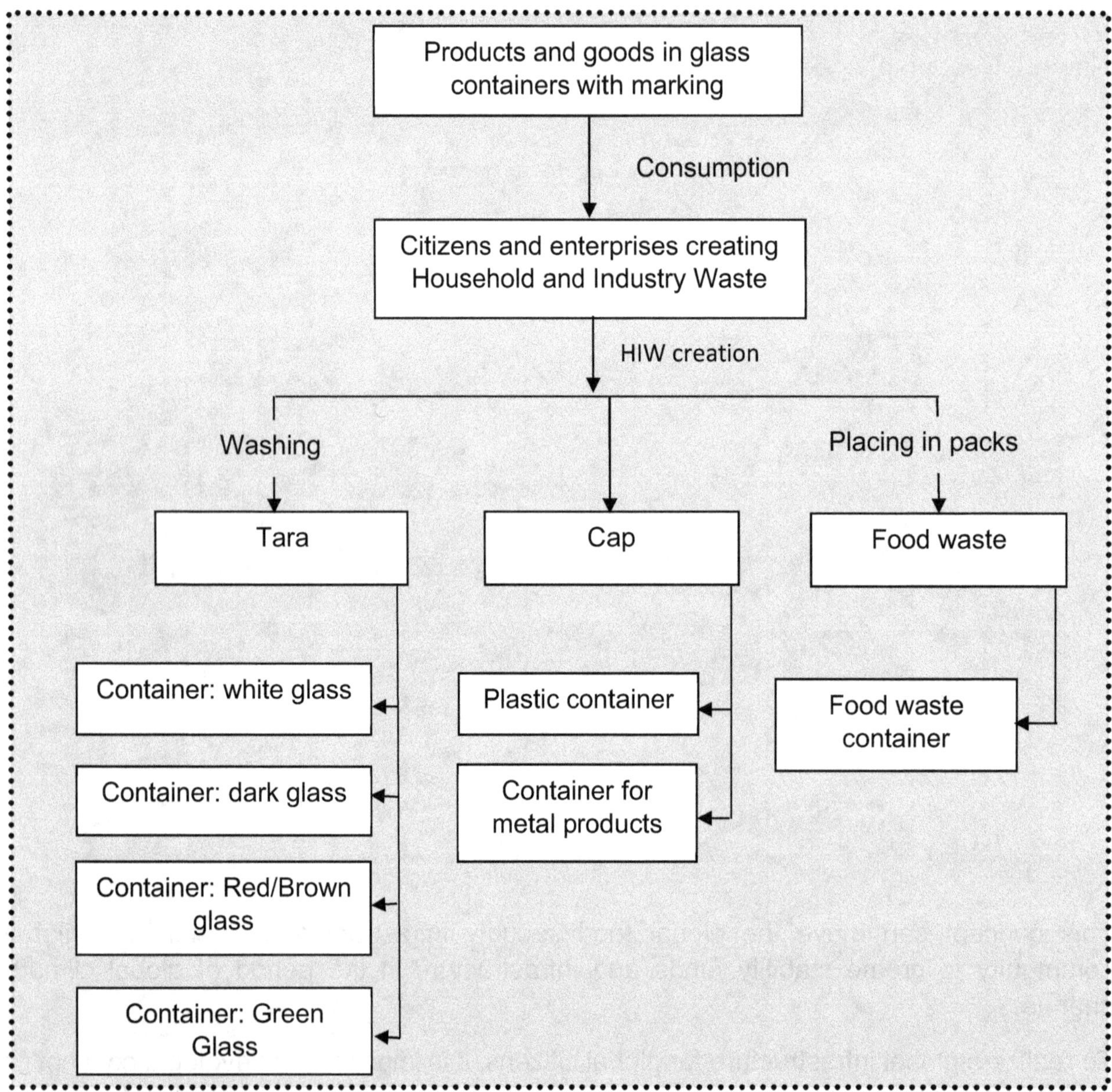

It does not work fast, as many points of the concept were far from understanding of local leaders. Without understanding the waste business, it is impossible to attract an investor.

Despite the fact that an idea was clear and I saw some progress in increasing the audience, investors were reluctant to join the waste business. Because locally, waste was something disgusting and associated with something dirty and smelly. It was hard to broke the stereotypes of the local mind. This requires time and another angle of vision to start with.

Generally, an ideal waste management system is a complex infrastructure, which can be launched only with a global mind. Figure 3 is one of the examples of the formation of waste by consumers.

When we take waste, from a regional point of view, there are some boundaries that limit countries to stop their financing for ecological and waste projects. That is because of the budget deficit. Therefore, in many countries, including in Central Asia, ecology and waste issues are getting their solutions very slowly.

Moreover, corruption and the absence of standards become the main barrier for protecting environmental programs. Let's take an example in the automotive industry. Today, many countries of Central Asia became a market of used cars with the lowest ecological standards. Millions of such cars on the roads are polluting environments without any legal requirements for ecological standards.

When we take into account the global infrastructure for ecology and waste, we have to understand that it requires building gradually an infrastructure. It is not possible to build a 100% zero waste infrastructure in one year or even 5 years. As it requires a strong educational and research institutions for constant information policies and training of population including children from kindergarten to up to old people, who handle waste every day.

Global Rights

Global Human Rights are a sensitive topic for many economies, especially with authoritarian, religious and dictatorship systems.

In many countries to protect human rights, the following institutions are working:

1) Lawyers;
2) Judges;
3) Public institutions;
4) NGOs;
5) Ombudsmen.

But on a regional and country-level, they are all dependent on government decisions and budgets. So, if the person really needs support about his or her violated human rights by the government or group of people, there is no way that these institutions will protect the citizens.

On the international level, the following communities are playing an important role:

1) Social Networks including Facebook, Instagram;
2) International Amnesty Organization;
3) United Nations Human Rights Organization;
4) International Lawyers;
5) International Organizations etc.

Nowadays, for example, Facebook and the International Amnesty Organization are much stronger institutions to protect the human rights of individuals in any country.

Global Citizens are one of the key citizens to whom not only the global infrastructure should work properly, but also, they are the key players in building global infrastructure for other citizens of our planet.

Only Global Citizens can provide right and appropriate solutions or actions for building a global infrastructure for waste and ecology management, protection of human rights or providing food security around the world.

It depends on many issues and factors, but the most important factor is the culture of Global Citizens. This factor will form true Global Citizens with a strong ideology for actions around the world.

Global Culture

Global Citizen is a person with a strong ideological position for the development of global communities through common actions.

Only Global Culture will be an indicator of the values and character of the Global Citizen and exemplary for other citizens. Via Global Culture, national citizens can understand the high values and missions of the Global Citizens and try to support them to join one day their row.

The global culture can be discussed from many points, but one of the key elements are the following:

-Citizenship;

-History;

-Values;

-Traditions;

-Religion;

-Thinking and Ideology.

Let me describe them below.

Citizenship

Citizenship is a legal proof of the citizen. It certifies to which territory a citizen belongs. But on a global scale, it has its own peculiarities. It cannot be based just on territorial belongings. Instead, the passport or identification document from the Global Government or Global Institutions should be issued based on a person's knowledge of languages, cultures, countries, and cultures and also personal history.

That means that Global Citizenship can be issued not from birth, but rather at the age of maturity.

Global Citizenship should be a legal document that can protect the rights of global citizens, open access to countries for greater contribution and actions and allow receiving benefits from global activities.

It is not clear who can issue this document or where it can be taken. But there should be a legal institution or government supported by world countries or global institutions.

Another good experience has Estonia, where they started to issue e-residency to any person from around the world several years ago. It can be in the same format for Global Citizenship in case of difficulty for creating a legal institution or issuing paper identification.

History

There are a lot of cases in history that can remote countries from each other and so from global unity. For example, in many countries of the post-soviet system, many ethnic groups do not like Russians or Chinese people because of their negative historical actions in the past, especially for mass killings and deportation of noble families.

The same to Iranians or North Koreans, who have absolutely outdated thinking about global issues and see the United States as a danger for their stability.

Historically, Iranians think that they are the only country where they link themselves to the prophet of the Mahomed. It is still preserved and they do not want to see Americans, British, French, Jews who they believe are the main enemy for Islam in the region.

But they totally do not understand that many Muslim diaspores are living in the US, UK, France and other countries of the world, including Islamic Banks which are first originated in the UK or other Western countries.

Probably, this is limited-mind thinking of people and the same about Iranians. And for sure there are many Iranians who are global citizens in heart and faith. The same in regard to Russians, Chinese and other nationalities.

In fact, Global Citizens should know not only the details of past history but also the reality of new history for global diversity and development. This is the only way how we can grow as human beings and global citizens.

It is impossible to live with a single ideology for progress. If there will be no competitive ideology there will be no rescue balloon from global tyranny.

The world should understand that no person can be killed because of race, color, nationality and so on. Imagine, if humans will try to eliminate one race. The effect can be dangerous for all other races. Because only with blood exchange between races, human beings are still strong and can survive in any weather conditions of the planet.

From a linkage point, one of the key points of genetical analysis is to find the links for the same ancestors. Today we have genetical analysis and some cultures preserved their tribal trees, which link one nationality to many cultures of the world.

It is important for the unity of the nations to include genetic test information into the global identification document and create a new history of humanity.

Many cultures and nationalities have the same values, traditions, and religions. They coexist as neighbor countries, but many divided by political games of the leading nations of the past. That's because leading countries try to manage other nations and they believe that they can.

For example, many Central Asian or Middle East countries have the same historical leaders and therefore have the same values, attitudes, and relationships in cultures.

For example, ethnic groups of Kazakhstan, Uzbekistan, Kyrgyzstan, Tajikistan, and Turkmenistan have the same national hero Alpamys. Many families read the tales of Alpamys to their children to grow them strong in faith and power, patriotic and gentlemen.

However, these countries have their new political systems with their own government and borders. And for global citizens, it is a way to approach to countries with the same values despite the differences in dialects and languages.

The same can be found on the global level. For example, many people read or saw Charles Dicken's stories or Peter Jackson's fantasy adventure film "The Lord of Rings". These are the films that formed many values of people, including modern etiquette in many spheres.

For Global Citizens, it is important to drive the nations for new actions via understanding their values and building new global values.

What the main global values of today? Let's list them below:

1) Honesty;
2) Fairness;
3) Goodwill;
4) Faithfulness;
5) Openness;
6) Respect others' rights
7) Love of freedom;
8) Respect for Equality;
9) Supportiveness;
10) Adventurous;
11) Respect of superiority of the knowledge;
12) Generosity;
13) Global mindset;
14) Others.

Global Citizen has to understand all the values of the character and try to promote them in other people.

Traditions

Only in Kazakhstan, we have more than 100 traditions which are specific only for the country. And there are also regional or rural traditions, which are specific only for the regions or cities.

The idea of the book is to create many new global traditions for global unity, exchange, communication, and development.

When we talk about global traditions, it should include the following traditions:

1) Debates;
2) Discussions;
3) Forums;
4) Brainstorming;
5) Contests;
6) Polls;
7) Feedbacks;
8) Meetings of various types;
9) Demonstrations;
10) Presentations;
11) How to do activities;
12) Investor Days;
13) Field workshops;
14) Parties;
15) Concerts;
16) Shows;
17) Interviews;
18) Actions;
19) Etc.

Global Traditions should allow global citizens to effectively communicate, interact and exchange with like-minded global and national citizens and also old-minded, or persons, who belong to a certain area. Traditions of global citizens should help to better understand each other and build truly global communities.

Religion

There are more than 100 religions around the world, and there are around 4 main directions or groups. From global understanding, we have to have a global religion with new values and power of God in absolutely new meaning and practices.

They should include the following new meaning and practices:

1) Reading books with learning critical thinking and creating new ideas;
2) Keep the appropriate rules and practices of main religions;
3) Start the actions and thanks to God in any global action, including in eating and sleeping;

4) Use effectively water, resources, and knowledge;
5) Help poorer and socially vulnerable people;
6) Promote global values, traditions, thinking, and religion;
7) Defend human rights, including of women and children;
8) Work, act, learn and teach with a passion for development global values;
9) Keep loyalty for global principles, values, traditions, and religion;
10) Stand strong for any ideas and offers against wars, corruption and other negative actions against humanity, nature, and peace;
11) Unite people for a single global religion of new deeds and actions;
12) Open and create future opportunities for all.

New global religion is not about praying and individual or group practices in the interest of religious groups, but rather it is a new way of thinking in the interest of good faith and the future.

Thinking and Ideology

Global Culture is a new global thinking approach and a new element of global ideology. It is impossible to implement a global culture without them.

Global Thinking is all about how global citizens think in different situations, especially in critical situations.

For example, in case of sudden war between countries, it is important for global citizens to protect the fairness and the rights of humans who have no relations to war parties. Or during a peaceful time, to defend the rights of socially vulnerable people, women or children.

Global ideology is based on the level of knowledge, experience, and actions about the global environment, culture, and politics. The ideology is stronger in the people, who have a wider knowledge of global history, politics, culture, etc.

And global ideology is one of the strongest tools for building appropriate global thinking in global citizens.

To expand global thinking and ideology in other communities and people, it is important to focus on global presence. It is about how the ideas are transferred to masses to help them understand the global thinking and ideology for all.

Global Presence

There are many ways for a global presence for any global citizen. In my book "200 web-sites and tools for online presence: the essential handbook for marketing and growth" I classified 200 web-sites and tools, which should help anyone to succeed in online presence. An approach of the book from a business point can be also applicable to global activities.

For a global citizen, it is important to do necessary steps for describing the processes and activities for global communities. This is a new way how other national citizens can be motivated and build interest for global actions.

Time and Mobility

Time is the most valuable resource for global citizens. It is important to understand the available time on a global scale for global actions.

At the same time, global mobility is a key element to involve global citizens in very urgent cases. For example, a global citizen of Kazakhstan with vast experience in the development of the country can move to another location, where he or she can easily contribute to the development of any other developing country in Asia, the Middle East, Africa, Central or South America.

The mobility of global citizens will create the best opportunities for a global presence.

Communication

Global Presence requires very strong communication skills and it is important to talk and speak to other people and connect effectively them with each other for common actions. In other words, for team building.

Therefore, it is not only about language or verbal skills, but also about negotiation, cultural, religious and NLP skills which are important to understand the decision-making processes of various cultural and ethnical groups.

Global citizens can improve communication skills only through communication and interaction both on a professional level and everyday level, including in building relationships for cooperation and achieving the same missions.

Global Actions

As a global citizen with a strong ideology for global development, it is time for global actions.

There are several ways to start global actions without any resources or capital. The only requirement is patience and consistent work on achieving the progress for global thinking.

Generally, the main requirements for global actions are:

-set a mission for global actions, for example, to change my region and make it first on the global map for new achievements;

-develop a positive attitude to achieve the mission;

-plan your global actions for each action with clear outcomes for the region, people and yourself;

-meet and communicate with people uniting them for global actions;

-implement global actions with leadership and responsibility about your region, people and offspring;

-present your ideas and mission clearly, receive feedback from team and audiences;

-evaluate your implemented global actions to make the next action more resultative.

These standard requirements are to follow the process. But it is also important to focus on content and personal skills.

The most influential instruments and tools for global actions are:

-interesting and continuous content;

-real facts from around the world;

-good speaking and presentation skills;

-audience involvement with feedback polls Q&A and interactions;

-statistics and comparisons of data;

-offering new ideas and projects for common action and others.

After meeting your audiences, they have to feel that they will act differently and they will change their principles for that.

Note that in many regions, people need more meetings to get the meaning for change. And the global citizen has to plan a long-term action plan.

As a fact, it is well-known that a person remembers only 30% of the information in 1 hour after the presentation. After one day - only 10% of it. And it requires to repeat 18-20 times to see the content to remember it for life. Therefore, the content generated by the global citizen should be:

1) Impressive;
2) Easy to remember;
3) Easy to imagine;
4) Easy to read and understand;
5) Accessible at any time via the internet

A global citizen should also understand that new content has to be presented 18-20 times, not in one year, but maybe in 5-10 years, depending on the complexity of the topic for global change.

In many cases, global citizens will be not easily understood by the audience and followers. Because followers will not usually act without financial support and without interest to achieve it quickly. Only achieving a mission can help the Global Citizen to find a way to sources of funding and investment. And only a mission will be a motivation to followers.

At the same time, a global citizen should understand at least 40-50 alternative sources of income to support his global actions on a constant base without financial resources or support.

The final point is how to cope with resistance from public or government officials. Many global actions will become a barrier for individuals and government officials to earn money from corrupted schemes or policies. They will show great resistance in many ways to destroy the plans of global citizens. They will try to involve public, youth and socially vulnerable groups of people to show their resistance.

Therefore, for global actions, it is important to consider targeted information strategies in various information channels and groups.

The Mission for Regional Change

Here in this section, I would like to show an example of a contribution to global change in one of the regions of Kazakhstan in the year 2018.

My missions for regional development started from the point to change the region and demonstrate its competitive advantages in a global arena.

For achieving a mission, I decided to involve international experts from one side and called for actions in many areas of international and regional collaboration, cooperation and activities.

Let me provide you with photo examples and how this helped to expand the horizons of local people.

17.01.2018 Organization of meetings and participation in the Kazakh-Portuguese Business Forum, Almaty city.

Organizing meetings with representatives of Portugal helped to see and evaluate the region's level of development in construction, agriculture, including in meat processing and greenhouse productivity.

25.01.2018 Meeting with entrepreneurs in Shymkent on investment project, RIC "Ontustik".

Meeting local businessmen and discussing various types of projects helped to motivate local businesses for global markets and development of tourism infrastructure.

06.03.2018 Meeting on the project development with youth, RIC "Ontustik".

Cooperation with the most active youth in the region helped the Regional Investment Center and generally the government to see the main problems of youth, especially those with global education.

15.03.2018 Business Meeting on the export of strawberries and other berries between the RIC "Ontustik" team and the Director of the Procurement Company from Russia.

Bringing a business procurement company with the farmers in one table provided many ideas for developing the agricultural sector in the region. It also helped to evaluate the main problems of agriculture compared to Turkey, Russia, Uzbekistan, and other Middle East countries.

17.03.2018 Organization of commodity exhibition for local producers and farmers, RIC "Ontustik".

The exhibitions and fairs helped to understand the level of preparedness of our businesses for exporting their products to the international markets.

We could also motivate our farmers to present their products and grow their businesses.

04.03.2018 Participation in the meeting with FoodSIB Company to export products to Siberia, Government of South-Kazakhstan region.

This meeting helped to understand new requirements and opportunities for farmers of the Turkestan region in Siberian markets.

20-30 март 2018 Presentations on the development of export potential in 16 districts and cities of South Kazakhstan Region.

My presentations in rural areas helped to evaluate the level of thinking in rural areas, understand the problems of farmers and their opportunities to grow.

9-11 April 2018 Promotion in the region the Annual Investment Meeting in Dubai: www.aimcongress.com

Participation in the promotion of the Annual Investment Meeting in Dubai helped me to understand that I can do business from any place in the world, even from rural areas. I had just needed internet access.

16.04.2018 Participation in Invest Day and meeting with a private investor Nurbek Rayev and young entrepreneurs, Chaplin Café.

Organization of meetings between investors and business people who need investment requires a lot of patience and understanding. But, the main lesson was that we could invite interested investors to Shymkent to evaluate local and rural projects from a different angle.

17.05.2018 Participation in the XI Astana Economic Forum with the participation of the Heads of States, Astana-EXPO, Astana city.

Participation in the annual Astana Economic Forum was an important lesson to evaluate the regional issues from a global expert view. In the sessions and meetings, I could find some of the solutions for regional and rural problems.

At the same time, I brought several institutions' attention to global thinking. I was participating in the forum as a member of the Regional Investment Center.

22.05.2018 The Business Forum of Kazakhstan and Uzbekistan, Meetings with leaders of international organizations, Zoodel and KazakhExport, Rixos Hotel Khadisha, Shymkent City.

Participation in the business forums and meetings with key people and institutions helped to attract the attention of Kazakh-Export to the regional projects. On the other side, we could evaluate and raise the topic of competitiveness of the farmers in Central Asia based on the competitive advantages of the countries and listing the products in the Zoodle Trade system.

19.05.2018 Round table on the development of a Green Economy in the South Kazakhstan region, M.Auezov South-Kazakhstan State University, Shymkent City.

The first time in the history prof. Raekwon Chung, A Green Policy Ambassador of South Korea in the United Nations Organizations visited the Turkestan Region and showed competitive advantages of the region for renewable energy sources. The conference could generally attract the attention of the region to new projects and sectors of the economy.

20.05.2018 Organization of Meeting for South-Korean Delegation with Akim and Deputy Akim of Turkestan city, Turkestan City.

During the visit, South-Korean Experts could meet the governors of the Turkestan Region and learn the potential of the region for solar and wind energy projects. Prof. Raekwon Chung could also see the situation in the waste landfills.

23.05.2018 Meeting with an exporter of safflower oil in Shymkent City.

Meeting with local exporter was very helpful to learn the main markets and barriers for developing the company. We also received a valuable recommendation and understanding of the level of technological development.

25.05.2018 Meeting with Prof. Kim Kwang Don, South-Kazakhstan State University.

The meetings at the university were very important to move the region to a new level of collaboration and development. Via feedback from prof. Kim Kwang Don, we could understand the real problems of universities in the regions.

05.06.2018 Organization of Meeting between Deputy Akim of Shymkent Mr. Timur Baymukhanov and Prof. Kim Kwang Don, Korean Expert in Construction and Concreate.

Connecting local government officials and representatives of the local university were very important to learn new projects and receive recommendations and ideas from an international expert.

07.06.2018 Meeting with Mr. David Cleve, Executive Director of the International Science and Technology Center and other interested parties in Astana.

Meetings with international experts are an important step to see regional issues from a different angle. International Science and Technology Center was one of the key organizers of the Renewable Energy Forum.

07.06.2018 Meeting with the head of the International Center for Green Technologies and Investment Projects Mr. Rapil Zhoshybayev in Astana city.

The development of the green sector of the Turkestan region requires a lot of effort over the main issues of policy development. Because on a regional level many processes and projects did not work well as planned.

09.06.2018 Meeting with ASTANA Innovations' Chairman of the Board Mr. Olzhas Sartayev, Astana City.

This meeting helped to see the plans of Astana city in the implementation of smart, eco and green technologies and compare it to the level of development in the regions and in South Korea.

07.06.2018~09.06.2018 Organization of the visit of the delegation from the region to the Summit Forum on Renewable Energy in Astana city.

Participation in the meetings and in the REW Forum helped me to see the main opportunities in the realization of the projects in the region.

At the same time, during the forums and discussions, it was clear that there are some unseen barriers on a central government level.

The most important part is a learning experience and collaboration with the local and international experts to find solutions for existing issues and policies.

12.06.2018 Meeting with Deputy Akim of Shymkent Mr. Timur Baymukhanov.

The meetings with heads of department of the Shymkent Government were organized to demonstrate a vision of the Korean expert Mr. Kim Kwang Don on city development issues and exchange ideas based on the development of Korean cities.

14.06.2018 Presentation on the topic of Shymkent Development to the directors of departments of the Government of Shymkent City.

Meetings and presentations in the Akimat of Shymkent helped to learn the level of state employees' thinking. It also helped to see the level of English Language and other cultural peculiarities.

28.06.2018 Memorandum signed between SKSU, RTC "Ontustik" and the Association for Ecological Organizations.

The memorandum is an important step to move relationships of local organizations to ecological and renewable projects.

28.06.2018 Organizing Meeting of the Director-General of the Department of International Cooperation of the Korea Environment Corporation Dr. You and Professor Raekwon Chung with the Akim of the Turkestan Region Mr. Zhanseit Tyuimebayev.

Prof. Raekwon Chung visited the region for the second time and invited Dr. You, a Director for International Cooperation of the K-Eco, a leading Korean organization for ecological projects.

28.06.2018 Organizing Meeting with Director-General of the Department of International Cooperation of the Korea Environment Corporation Dr. You and Professor Raekwon Chung with Shymkent Akim Mr. Gabidulla Abdrahimov and at the Shymkent Agrarian College.

With the delegation from Korea, we visited the Turkestan Higher Agrarian College – a main educational center for the preparation of specialists for the agrarian sector. This provided a ground to see future perspectives for starting projects with the college.

01.07.2018~03.07.2018 Organizing Meeting of Deputy Chairman of RIC "Ontustik" within the Forum of Mayors of Cities of the Silk Road countries - GLOBAL SILK ROAD in Astana city.

With delegation from Regional Investment Center and South-Kazakhstan State University, we participated in the Silk Road Forum of Mayors of cities in Astana City.

We have met with experts and governors of the cities from Europe and Asia. They were interested to visit Shymkent city and Turkestan region as it was in the center of the Silk Road. It was important for us to announce the new opportunities in the region with the new status of the Turkestan region and Shymkent city.

Mayors of Estonian cities showed interest in the transfer of the EU experience in the implementation of the smart city projects in the Turkestan region and Shymkent city.

01.07.2018~03.07.2018 Organizing Meetings of Deputy Chairman of the RIC "Ontustik" within the Forum of Mayors of Cities of the Silk Road countries - GLOBAL SILK ROAD in Astana city

In the forum, leading managers of our organization could learn new technologies, which help farmers and agrarians to manage and monitor large territories with small flying objects – drones. They could also use them in spraying fertilizers and monitoring for watering, observations and etc.

The meetings and sessions were fruitful to change the thinking of our managers. They could learn new ideas and concepts for implementing projects in the region.

During the discussions, international experts showed special interests in the implementation of waste management projects in the region.

10.07.2018 Organizing Meeting with the participation of «JV Robo Avia» and SKSU.

The aim of the Regional Investment Center was to help private companies, which had new technology, to link with university research centers. It was not so easy. But we tried to do the first steps in the region.

13.07.2018 Organizing Meeting between representatives of the Department of Architecture of the Shymkent Government and the Korean company HEERIM.

Our aim at the Regional Investment Center was to involve as many Korean companies in the work of building a new Turkestan city. We tried to learn what are new technologies in the market.

17.07.2018 Appointed as an Advisor to Shymkent Agrarian College, Turkestan Higher Agrarian College.

I was motivated to join Turkestan Higher Agrarian College as an Advisor to the Director. This helped me to join the college and interact with teachers and students for a better understanding of the level of development of educational and practical processes.

Another main idea was to understand the quality of education. As a member of the Regional Investment Center, which finances businesses in the agro sector, I was interested to know about the level of preparation of agrarian specialists.

20.07.2018~23.07.2018 Evaluating Laboratories of South-Kazakhstan State University.

As a representative of the Regional Investment Center, I was interested to know about the level of development of the laboratories of the research centers and universities and how they can help our clients, financed in the RIC.

The main idea was to connect businesses, research centers and universities in one single process of development of new products and services.

30.07.2018 Memorandum signed between SKSU and Korean Concrete Institute, South-Kazakhstan State University.

30.07.2018 Memorandum was signed between SKSU, RIC "Ontustik" and the Korean Concrete Institute, South-Kazakhstan State University.

The idea of signing memorandums was to start new collaboration and projects with universities and Korean partners.

The memorandum could help the Regional Investment Center to see new areas of cooperation in construction, green technologies, city and high building technologies.

30.07.2018 Memorandum signed between SKSU, RIC "Ontustik" and LLP "JV RoboAvia", South-Kazakhstan State University.

With our efforts, we could also bring RoboAvia to cooperate with the university on new elements of the products.

30.07.2018 Organizing Meeting of the delegation from KCI with the Chairman of the Board of the RIC "Ontustik" Mr. Kuanysh Baytore.

30.07.2018 Organizing Meeting of the delegation from the KCI with the Deputy Akim of Shymkent Mr. Bauyrzhan Mamyraliev.

In the region, I could also organize a meeting of the Korean delegation in the Office of the Deputy Governor of the Shymkent City. As a participant of the meeting, I could understand the issues in the construction sector of the city as well as difficult channels of communication.

August 2018 Development of www.mep.kz, a project for the export development office of the Akimat of Turkestan region.

In August of 2018, we could launch our electronic information system for farmers and exporters of the region. It provided prices about agro-products in the region. On the other hand, we developed a system, that explained businesses how effectively export products to various destinations.

08.08.2018 Organizing Meeting with prof. Kim Kwang Don in the RIC "Ontustik".

We had been meeting with prof. Kim Kwang Don once in a week to discuss various issues of the development of the regional economy. One of the key topics: "how to change the thinking of local people?".

We wrote and discussed many strategies and tried to write reports based on analysis and discussions.

Many reports and recommendations, I could send to the President Office, Government of Kazakhstan, Governors of the Region, top managers of the universities, colleges and our Regional Investment Center.

The recommendations included the following sectors:

1) Support of SMB;
2) Development of regional and rural areas;
3) Implementation of green projects;
4) Development of Export Potential and Investment Climate of the Region etc;

23.08.2018~25.08.2018 Organizing Meetings about the investment projects and for signing a memorandum between SKSU, RIC "Ontustik", SHINSUNG E&G and "ON EXPORT" LLP.

Thanks to Prof. Raekwon Chung, our Region was visited by a representative of the leading solar company in Korea "Shinsung E&G".

We could organize a meeting with interested sides in the region and also show the region's opportunities for the installation of solar electrical stations.

At the same time, the local sides could understand the requirements and the main barriers to the implementation of solar projects.

24.08.2018 Organizing Tour for participation in Melonfest in Zhetysay city.

With Korean experts, we attended also a number of exhibitions, forums, and fairs in the region to learn the main products of the region and to evaluate the export potential with regional main barriers.

12.09.2018 Organizing Meeting at the Research and Production Center for grain farming in the Nauchniy.

To learn the experience in agro research, I visited the Nauchyi region in the Akmola region to learn the experience of the organization.

18.09.2018 Organizing Lectures in Shymkent Agrarian College on the topics: Innovative activity of the college through innovation, export, and competitiveness of the agricultural sector of the region and Shymkent city.

As an Advisor of the Director of the Turkestan Higher Agrarian College, I could organize weekly seminars with the participation of staff and students. I prepared presentations and speeches to change the local mindset and motivate local students for greater contributions.

My topics included the development of educational and research processes until the development of the export potential of the region in agriculture and agribusiness.

September 2018, teaching in SKSU topics: Competitiveness and Management, Project Management and Marketing Communication.

With the support of the rector and vice-rectors of South-Kazakhstan State University, I could start my lectures to prepare and change marketing and management students.

In various semesters, I was lecturing in Marketing Communication, Marketing and Competitiveness and Project Management.

18.09.2018 Organizing Meeting on project's implementation in SKSU M.Auezova.

To attract investments for building new campus buildings (dormitory, sports facilities, swimming pool, etc.), we were organizing meetings to see how we can contribute to the development of the project.

12.11.2018 Organizing Presentation of projects in Agrocollege of Turkestan region.

To support students' initiatives and projects, we organized special presentation days of students with participation of the top management of the Regional Investment Center. My aim was to connect the Regional Investment Center to support startup projects of students. I believed that they can be more productive and fast-growing in the future.

12.11.2018 Award ceremony of certificates for the best project initiators, the Agrocollege of Turkestan region.

The best projects of students, we awarded with certificates for the next level of competition and possible financial support from the Regional Investment Center.

10.11.2018 Collaboration in Days of France in Kazakhstan, Rixos Hotel.

To attract investments from various countries and also promote the local products for exports, we collaborated with local representatives of the embassies and international organizations such as EBRD, ADB, Ambassadors and other international experts.

15.11.2018 Organization of the presentation of students of SKSU in the RIC "Ontustik".

To motivate my students of SKSU, I organized their participation in our internal staff meetings about financing projects or their realization.

28.11.2018 Organization and participation in the V International Conference of Engineering and Technology, South-Kazakhstan State University.

At university, I organized and participated in international conferences to listen to speakers about new technologies, ideas, and developments in various fields of industries. I also presented my concepts on the development of export potential, the attraction of investments and financing projects in the rural and regional industries.

29.11.2018 Organization of a Meeting with engineers from South Korea, Kazavtodor.

I tried to participate in various meetings with the participation of international businessmen and experts to receive their feedbacks on main barriers for development, thinking and opportunities to grow.

30.11.2018 Participation in the round table on the topic of Mustafa Chokai.

We actively involved the youth, businesses, and students in various open discussion meetings, organized in the atmosphere of nice creativeness, books and evening snacks.

We have discussed topics of history, business projects, stock markets, and other key areas.

08.12.2018 Participation in the Shymkent Development Forum, Rixos Hotel.

It was an important event organized by the Shymkent Government with a number of key speakers from around the world. It was the first step to move the city to a new level of events.

25.12.2018 Organization and participation in the Agriculture Conference, South-Kazakhstan State University.

Turkestan has a sunny region which has lured climate for agriculture and agri-business industries. We organized a number of conferences and round tables on this topic, including with EBRD experts, in the SKSU and private investors.

Conclusion

Increasing the number of global citizens requires many efforts and areas to develop.

We have to understand that this is not a one-year process, rather it is a constant work and long-term action.

In this book, I tried to explain my own story of being a global citizen on a regional level and share it with those who can extract valuable lessons for future contributions.

Being a global citizen is not something you have to learn every day or read thousands of books to contribute, it is a character of sharing good values and actions, which can become a global one.

I call my readers and many interested citizens with a global mindset for cooperation and collaboration. There are many ways to do research and develop new tools and solutions for global citizenship.

Feel free to contact me for your ideas and comments via email at nurbek2020@gmail.com

About author

Nurbek Achilov is a global citizen with more than 20 years of experience in international activities, forums, and events. He holds a Visionary Level on Global Citizen Platform with his over 100 global actions to support global leaders.

He is involved as a lecturer of marketing and management at South-Kazakhstan State University where he focuses on the preparation of students with global orientations in marketing, management, and other disciplines.

Nurbek is a founder of several organizations and projects in several countries. He enjoys writing about multiple issues of the global economy and development. As a member of educational institutions, he understands well about the problems of the global economy and development. He explores many areas on how to improve the situation to help the regions to adapt to the international level.

Nurbek Achilov has some resources for you!

On Blogger's platform, he runs his blog about investments, export, trade, and other issues.

Blog about investment, export, and trade in English:

https://nurbekachilov.blogspot.com/

Blog about investment, export, and trade in English:

https://nurbekachil.blogspot.com/

You can also find ideas, photos, and experiences about investments, trade and investment on Nurbek Achilov's pages on Facebook, Instagram, Pinterest, Slideshare, Academia and LinkedIn and other accounts.

orcid.org/0000-0003-1238-6556

Kazakhstan

Tips for Travelers

Nurbek Achilov

Second Edition

2019

200 web-sites and tools for online presence

Essential Handbook for marketing and growth

Nurbek Achilov

First Edition

2019

Get my new book with the Special Price on Amazon.com

Waste Management

From Concept till Action Plan

Nurbek Achilov

First Edition

2010

Get this new book with the Special Price on Amazon.com

500 Motivating and Inspiring Quotes

Discovering Great Leaders and People

Nigel Aksel

1st Edition, 2019

Market Trends

Historical Data

Nigel Aksel

Second Edition, 2019